WHAT'S COMING NEXT?

WHAT ABOUT THE VACCINE?

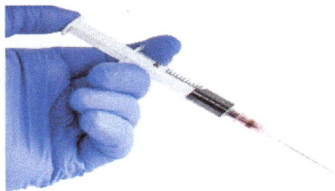

REL067030: Religion: Christian Theology –
Apologetics.

ISBN 978-1-7371005-1-5

All Scripture quotes are from the King James Bible.

THE OLD PATHS PUBLICATIONS, Inc.
142 Gold Flume Way
Cleveland, Georgia, U.S.A. 30528

Web: www.theoldpathspublications.com
E-mail: TOP@theoldpathspublications.com

TABLE OF CONTENTS

UNPRECEDENTED THINGS HAPPENING

During 2020, we all witnessed and experienced unprecedented things happening, not just in our local areas, but worldwide. People panicked and felt so confused, as no one seemed to have any real answers to the problems we were facing.

WE WERE TOLD...

Due to this so-called 'pandemic', we were told hundreds of thousands of people died, but did they really die *because of* **COVID**-19? Did more people die than usual this year?

Do your own research. When a bad dose of the **flu** hits, many elderly and vulnerable people succumb to it. So, did more people die this year *because of* **COVID-**19 compared to other years with the **flu**? *Do your own research*, as it's quite startling to say the least. I just typed into Google one question about the amount of people who die each year of the **flu** and compared the figures, I would suggest you do the same and see for yourselves.

So, did more people really die in 2020 than usual because of this Coronavirus?

WHAT OTHER IMPACT?

What other impact has this so-called pandemic had on us?

Millions of people have lost their jobs and the worldwide economy *nose dived* at a rapid rate seldom ever seen. Think of the consequences of this, short and long-term. Have you been affected by it regarding your employment? Do you know someone who has?

DEVASTATING AFTERMATH

The aftermath of all this has been devastating, with even more confusion and anxiety among everyone, no one is at peace, and a lot worse is coming sadly.

The instigation of wearing mandatory face masks in many places has driven a social divide among people, many no longer want to be around others, the human race has certainly parted ways. Someone wants to condition, desensitise, and control us it seems. If *they* can get you to wear a face mask, what else can *they* get you to do?

The 'old world' is being phased out and a 'new norm' is being introduced, and everyone, like sheep, is going along with it.

This whole situation is still all very surreal and bizarre, stop and think about what has *actually* happened, and what the next step *could* be. Have you any idea?

WHERE DOES SOMEONE TURN?

In a worldwide crisis, where do people turn to for help, for truth, and for answers?

The majority, again like sheep, followed 'Government Guidelines', yet even the Government itself was in disarray through all of this, and oftentimes was clueless, not knowing what to do. It was chaotic to say the least.

There used to be a thing called 'Freedom of the Press' – it meant the right to report news or circulate opinion without censorship from the Government and was considered 'one of the great bulwarks of liberty, by the Founding Fathers of the United States. Americans enjoy freedom of the press as one of the rights guaranteed by the First Amendment. But it's not like that anymore in the USA or in the UK. There is no such thing as 'Freedom of the Press' anymore, the Media is just propaganda for those private companies and 'elites' who own them. If you want the truth, do not turn to the media for answers.

So where can we go to find *absolute truth?* Now there's a question, and one I will answer shortly.

We are all still experiencing uncertain times, and many people are very anxious as to what is really happening. The majority, as always, just follow the current trend, and just like the people did in the 1930's by being duped into voting Adolf Hitler into power, the majority will be deceived and also fall for *what is coming*. Something sinister is happening behind the scenes and something big is just over the horizon. (Note as an example, the majority of people have fallen for the lie of 'evolution'. Most people *think* evolution is scientific, when in reality it's a religion, a belief system, *everything* coming from *nothing* is impossible. You were created by God, you were designed. To get from a single cell to a complex human being over billions of years, is utterly ridiculous, it's nonsense, yet it's taught *as fact* in schools to our children. This is deception and delusion at its very best. Have you been sucked in by it?)

HAVE YOU ANY IDEA WHAT IS COMING NEXT?

CONFUSED AND CONTROLLED

I found it quite incredible, how overnight, the people (us), were being contained and controlled – don't leave your house; don't drive to the next town, *if you do*, you'll be sent back or arrested. We were even stopped from seeing our family members, suddenly we all had to adhere to a list of '*do's and don'ts* – it was forced upon us, and if you broke these 'unlawful laws', like visiting your mother on her deathbed, you would be punished, even imprisoned. Many people equated this to Nazi Germany in the 1930's and 40's.

This was all done in the name of 'Government Guidelines' for safety... contain, quarantine and control. We were told that we're in a pandemic and this Coronavirus is killing thousands... but was it... did it... is it? *Do your own research, you'll be amazed.* Someone is lying to us.

Day after day we were bombarded with so-called 'facts and figures', yet these were conflicting and inconsistent in many instances as to what was *actually* happening. Special mobile hospitals were being set up in huge venues around the country, but never used. If you were 'healthy' there was a 99% chance you would recover if you caught **COVID-**19 (doesn't that sound like the **flu**?) Children were 99% safe from it and hardly a child died *because of it*, yet all the schools were shut down, and everyone was told to work from home. This also caused a tremendous number of problems in itself.

When everyone was ordered to stay at home, and told not to drive *anywhere*, I wonder what *they* were doing behind our backs? Have you noticed anything new erected on your street, in your town, or on motorways recently, or is this just 'conspiracy?' Something *has* happened, and something *is* coming very soon, but what?

We also saw doctors and scientists saying opposite things to one another, so who can we trust?

If you stand against the 'norm' today, oftentimes you are silenced through censorship. If you speak out against so-called 'authorities' e.g. the Government, the medical profession, people in power etc., suddenly you find your YouTube account taken down... there is no such thing as 'free speech', you're not even allowed to have an opinion today without the fear of getting into trouble or even being arrested.

HERE ARE QUESTIONS TO PONDER

How/Why on earth did 'most people' vote Adolf Hitler into power; how did he get into that position? *Think long and hard about that.* Could this situation happen again?   Could history repeat itself?

IF the Government can stop you FROM visiting your relative on their deathbed; IF *they* can force you to stay at home and not cross over the border into another town; IF *they* can stop you getting married or attend a funeral; IF *they* can get you to wear a face mask, even though the face mask has been proven *not* to be effective with this kind of virus, WHAT ELSE can *they* get you to do?

Most people will queue up for 'the vaccine' especially if they make it mandatory, without *even questioning* what is actually in the substance.   They will allow themselves to be pumped full of unknown chemicals, without even questioning what it will do to them or what the complications or side effects will be. They will do what they are told, believing it to be right. *"**There is a way which seemeth right unto a man, but the end thereof are the ways of death**."* Proverbs 14v12. Many people *think* they know what is right, when, it is wrong. Do you *know* what is in the vaccine you are being injected with?

Many people who have taken vaccines or drugs have suffered greatly in later life from all kinds of debilitating illnesses that have been linked to vaccines or drugs (do your own research and start by looking up 'Thalidomide' as an example). Be incredibly careful what you allow your body to be injected with, as it's unnatural.

SO WHY THE RANT?

Because what is happening is wrong, and time is running out. We need people 'shouting from the rooftops' telling the truth so everyone will stop and think before walking as a sheep to the slaughter.

There is a verse found in the King James Bible which says this... **"And judgment is turned away backward, and justice standeth afar off: for truth is fallen in the street, and equity cannot enter."** Isaiah 59v14. How true this is.

I'm just trying to get you to think 'outside of the box' as they say, as not everything is as it seems, big trouble is coming.

Change one letter in the word 'ma**s**k' and you have the word 'ma**r**k'. Today, you can only shop if you are wearing a 'mask'... tomorrow will come when you will only be able to shop if you have 'the mark'... **"And that no man might buy or sell, save he that had the mark, or the name of the beast, or the number of his name."** Revelation 13v17. **("Here is wisdom. Let him that hath understanding count the number of the beast: for it is the number of a man; and his number is Six hundred threescore and six."** Revelation 13v18).

Isn't it interesting that over the last few years we've seen a huge surge in tattoos and piercings, yet look at what the Bible says in regard to this... **"Ye shall not make any cuttings in your flesh..., nor print any marks upon you: I am the LORD."** Leviticus 19v28. Why is there such a fascination of having your skin 'marked', or your flesh 'pierced'? *Something is coming very soon...!*

THE BIBLE TELLS US

The Bible tells us what the future holds for all of us, yet the majority of people, as always, like sheep, have rejected the word of God and gone their own way instead, and that is sin.

"For all have sinned..." Romans 3v23. *"For the wages of sin is death; but the gift of God is eternal life through Jesus Christ our Lord."* Romans 6v23.

"And ye have this day rejected your God, who himself saved you out of all your adversities and your tribulations; and ye have said unto him, Nay, but set a king over us..." 1 Samuel 10v19.

THE ANTICHRIST

People have rejected the Lord Jesus Christ, and instead, they will follow a new 'king', and that 'king' is coming very soon. He is known in the Bible as the Antichrist. You may not believe this, but if you are not following the Lord Jesus Christ, you shall follow His enemy without realising or understanding it. Read Revelation chapter 13 in a King James Bible for some insight.

The entire world is in a mess and very soon, someone will arise who will seem to have all the answers, and the majority of people will not only follow him, they will worship him, just like they did with Adolf Hitler.

A WAY TO BE SAVED

There is a way to be saved from all of what is to come, and it's by putting your faith and trust in Jesus Christ as your Saviour. You and I are sinners bound for Hell, but because of His incredible love for us, Jesus Christ took our sins, died, and was judged in our place. Three days later He arose from the dead and is now seated in Heaven with His Father. Very soon, the Lord Jesus Christ shall return and gather up every Christian to Himself and take them back to their new home in Heaven. If you turn to Him right now, asking Him to forgive you for all your sins, you shall be saved immediately and counted in this group.

SEVEN YEARS OF TRIBULATION

If not, you will have to endure seven years of tribulation like this world has never seen (Matthew 24v21). You can read about what will happen during this time in Revelation chapters 5 – 19, which concludes with the Battle of Armageddon. For some comfort, read chapters 20-22 and see how it all ends. You are either a child of God or a child of the Devil, there is no middle ground. You either believe the Gospel (the death, burial and resurrection of the Lord Jesus Christ – 1 Cor 15v1-4, Col 1v14, Eph 2v8+9, Gal 3v21-29, Titus 3v5, Rom 10v4, Rom 7v4, Gal 5v4, Gal 2v16, Gal 3v11, John 3v16+18+36), or you reject His word and go your own way, all of which has devastating consequences. The choice is yours.

"Also I set watchmen over you, saying, Hearken to the sound of the trumpet. But they said, We will not

hearken. Therefore hear, ye nations, and know, O congregation, what is among them. Hear, O earth: behold, I will bring evil upon this people, even the fruit of their thoughts, because they have not hearkened unto my words, nor to my law, but rejected it." Jeremiah 6v17-19.

"The wise men are ashamed, they are dismayed and taken: lo, they have rejected the word of the LORD; and what wisdom is in them?" Jeremiah 8v9. Without the Lord there is no hope, "as the truth is in Jesus" (Eph 4v21).

"But the Pharisees and lawyers rejected the counsel of God..." Luke 7v30. If you want to know the truth read the **King James Bible**. If you reject the word of God, you become self-righteous and believe you know better than God does (Luke 18v9, Luke 16v15, 1 Sam16v7, Phil 3v9, Isa 64v6, Rom 10v3, 2 Pet 2v10+12-18, Job 32v1+2, Job 35v2). Whether prince or pauper you need Jesus Christ as your Saviour. Without God, you are without hope (Eph 2v12).

FURTHER READING

What the Bible says about rejecting the word of God – Isa 5v24, Num 15v31, 2 Chron 36v16, Amos 2v4, 1 Sam 15v23, 2 Kings 17v15, Jer 6v19, 2 Kings 22v8+11+13 (2 Kings 23v1-3), (Ps 12v6+7), Ps 107v11, Jer 13v10, Jer

16v12, read all of 2 Kings 17 and Jer 36. There is no hope for you at all if you reject the word of God, the King James Bible.

"But God hath chosen the foolish things of the world to confound the wise; and God hath chosen the weak things of the world to confound the things which are mighty; And base things of the world, and things which are despised, hath God chosen, yea, and things which are not, to bring to nought things that are: That no flesh should glory in his presence. But of him are ye in Christ Jesus, who of God is made unto us wisdom, and righteousness, and sanctification, and redemption: That, according as it is written, He that glorieth, let him glory in the Lord." 1 Cor 1v27-31 (1 Cor 3v18-21, 1 Cor 2v14, 2 Tim 3v7, Rom 1v22, 1 Cor 1v18+19, James 2v5).

TIME IS RUNNING OUT

Time is running out... you need to get saved, become a Christian, having all your sins forgiven by the Lord Jesus Christ. It is then and only then, you will understand the meaning of life.

The end is coming, but before it does, there is a person who will rise up and take control of the world. People will be deceived into thinking that he is God, but he isn't, he is

'The Antichrist'. He will seek to befriend Israel and all Jews everywhere, but in reality, he will try to destroy Israel until Israel's Saviour comes at His Second Coming, the Lord Jesus Christ. He will destroy all His enemies and set up His 'Kingdom on Earth', it will be known as the Millennial Reign of Jesus Christ, the Kingdom of Heaven on Earth.

This booklet is written as a warning, giving you a glimpse of what is just around the corner. What you do with this truth is up to you, but if I were you, I'd get saved right now where you are before it's too late.

...what must I do to be saved? ...Believe on the Lord Jesus Christ, and thou shalt be saved... Acts 16:30+31.

"In whom we have redemption through his blood, even the forgiveness of sins:" Colossians 1v14.

The Vaccine

They've changed the word 'Flu' to 'Covid'

...and the whole world 'bought it!'

Now 'they' are telling us that the answer is...

Do your own research and check out the figures. We are NOT in any kind of 'Pandemic'.

There are 66,650,000 people in the UK. Less than 0.2% died of the Flu aka Covid19 in 2020.

That is NOT a pandemic!

How many people usually die of the Flu each year? (Go back over the last 10 years).

Now look up how many people have died... 'because of' Covid (Flu) rather than died 'WITH' Covid (Flu).

Something is wrong!

1. Suddenly the Flu doesn't exist anymore...!? Wake up people!

2. Wearing a mask is a waste of time and not scientifically proven.

I repeat, something is wrong! We are all being *bullied* by the government, police, and local authorities regarding 'lockdowns', social distancing, wearing face masks, visiting each other... we aren't even allowed to visit our dying loved ones.

3. 'They' are also destroying our businesses, livelihoods, families, and mental health.

It needs to STOP right NOW!

Imagine a vaccine so safe,

1. You have to be 'threatened' to take it.
2. *For a disease so 'deadly,' you have to be 'tested' to know whether you've even got it!*

If I get vaccinated...

1. Can I stop wearing the mask? Government says –**No**
2. Can we reopen all the shops and restaurants and everyone work normally again? Government says – **No**
3. Will I be resistant to Covid? Government says -**Maybe, but we**

don't know exactly, it probably won't stop you getting it.

4. At least I won't be contagious to others anymore? Government says –**No, you can still pass it on, possibly, nobody knows.**

5. If I am vaccinated, can I stop social distancing? Government –**No**

6. If I am vaccinated, can I stop disinfecting my hands? Government – **No**

7. If I vaccinate myself and my grandparents, can we hug each other? Government –**No**

8. Will cinemas, theatres and stadiums operate as normal thanks to vaccines? Government –**No**

9. What is the benefit of the vaccine? Government Response - **Hoping the virus won't kill you.**

10. Are you sure it won't kill me? Government says **– No**

11. If statistically the virus won't kill me anyway (99.7% survival rate) ... Why would I get vaccinated?" Government Response - **To protect others.**

12. So, if I get vaccinated, I can protect 100% of people that I come in contact with? Government says -**No**

13.   Can you guarantee that I won't experience adverse side-effects from taking the vaccine, or even die from the vaccine itself?   Government Response - **No**

14.   Since you're encouraging everyone to get vaccinated, if people do experience adverse reactions, or even die from the vaccine, will they or their families   be   compensated? Government response –**No - the Government and vaccine manufactures have 100% zero liability.**

To Summarise

So, to summarise, the Covid19 vaccine...

1. Does **NOT** give immunity.
2. Does **NOT** eliminate the virus.
3. Does **NOT** prevent death.
4. Does **NOT** guarantee you won't get it.
5. Does **NOT** stop you passing it on.
6. Does **NOT** eliminate the need for travel bans.
7. Does **NOT** eliminate the need for business closures.
8. Does **NOT** eliminate the need for lockdowns.

9. Does **NOT** eliminate the need for wearing masks.

So, my question is... 'What is the point of getting the vaccine?'

Supermarket 'police' (aka 'minions in fluorescent high vis vests') *suddenly feeling important***, are persecuting those who DON'T wear a mask. I would suggest writing to the manager explaining 'your rights' and even suing those who 'harass' you. If you don't stand up NOW, worse will come. This is like Nazi Germany without the violence... yet!**

Next time you feel like praising the NHS read this first and imagine if YOU were in this situation...

Man's family 'begged' for hospital visit before he died

A woman has described how she 'begged' in vain to see her husband before he died in hospital.

David Howells, 57, spent two weeks on wards at Nottingham City Hospital after being admitted with complications relating to a heart condition.

Exemptions to Covid restrictions allow for some compassionate visits, but Mr Howells' wife Sharon and daughter Kim's requests were refused.

The hospital trust said it believed its policies (!!!) were applied correctly. (!!!)

Mrs Howells, 58, said: "What we can never forget, understand or forgive, is the fact he was denied any contact even in his darkest, scariest moments of life."

Mr Howells had the "fighting spirit taken out of him" in hospital, said his wife. Mr Howells, a father of three, was admitted to hospital in January with complications caused by a condition known as Cardiomyopathy.

However, his health did not improve. He also tested positive for Coronavirus (!!!), which his family believe he picked up in hospital.

Mr Howells' wife said he sent them texts and videos showing he was struggling mentally and physically, and that they 'begged' doctors to see him.

At one point Mrs Howells said she and her daughter Kim were on a ward just feet away, but were not allowed any further.

'It was cruel'. She said she accepted it may not have been considered an 'end of life' situation, but that she was told there was a 'good chance' he would not return home.

"If this was not a compassionate situation, what is?" she asked. "Had we been allowed just five minutes with him under supervision, he would still be here."

"The fighting spirit was taken out of him."

"It was cruel, it shouldn't have happened."

Mr Howells died of heart failure on 8 February, after sending a final text.

It read: "I'm really not good. I don't think I'm going to make it. They're not listening."

His family were called in as his health deteriorated, but were not able to get there in time, despite Mrs Howells rushing to the hospital in her pyjamas.

This poor family. What a tragic situation, my heart breaks for them. Idiot doctors and nurses destroying families through disgusting and despicable decisions. The **NHS** on the whole is excellent, but things like this are deplorable, especially when I think it could have been me in that situation with my wife or children. The leaders of our Government, and those who are in authority everywhere, have a lot to answer for regarding this FAKE pandemic. Millions of people are struggling financially and mentally because of the horrendous decisions our 'leaders' are making, and millions will die if something is NOT done about it NOW.

Why isn't mainstream media covering all the protests that are taking place?

Why all the censorship? What are 'they' hiding and withholding from us all?

If you don't start standing up <u>from today</u>, it will get much worse.

ADDITIONAL READING

If you really want the truth, start reading some of these people/articles below and spread the word...

<u>Covid-19: The Greatest Hoax in History</u> by Vernon Coleman (UK)

<u>Proof That Face Masks Do More Harm Than Good</u> by Vernon Coleman (UK)

<u>Vernon Coleman</u> – up to date medical truths about vaccines, face masks, anti-social distancing, and more (UK)

<u>Dolores Cahill</u> – Molecular Biologist/Immunologist speaking out against what is happening in this world (UK)

Sherri J. Tenpenny website with scientific articles exposing vaccine myths and pharma foibles (USA)

UK Column – for truthful news (UK)
www.thehighwire.com

Hugo Talks – good video commentary on the daily news (UK)

The Light Paper – a free monthly truth paper (UK)

Newsmax and **OANN** – for truthful non-fake news coverage (USA)

Richie Allen – covering the news the mainstream media won't (UK)

SOMETHING SINISTER IS LURKING IN THE SHADOWS.

Soon 'a beast' shall arise and the world will follow him!

(Read Revelation 13 in a King James Bible)

...I declare unto you the gospel ...Christ died for our sins according to the scriptures; And that he was buried, and that he rose again the third day according to the scriptures: 1 Corinthians 15v1-4.

...Believe on the Lord Jesus Christ, and thou shalt be saved... Acts 16v31.

For there is one God, and one mediator between God and men, the man Christ Jesus. 1 Timothy 2v5.

For God so loved the world, that he gave his only begotten Son, that whosoever believeth in him should not perish, but have everlasting life. John 3v16.

In whom we have redemption through his blood, even the forgiveness of sins. Colossians 1v14.

Trust in the LORD with all thine heart; and lean not unto thine own understanding. In all thy ways acknowledge him, and he shall direct thy paths. Be not wise in thine own eyes: fear the LORD, and depart from evil. Proverbs 3v5-7.

WHEN DO I BECOME A CHRISTIAN?

WHEN DO YOU BECOME A
CHRISTIAN?

You become a Christian the moment you quit trusting your own righteousness to get you to Heaven, and start trusting the righteousness of JESUS CHRIST!

For he hath made him to be sin for us, who knew no sin; that we might be made the righteousness of God in him.
2 Corinthians 5:21

Romans 5v8

But God commendeth his love toward us, in that, while we were yet sinners, Christ died for us.

Romans 3v23
For all have sinned, and come short of the glory of God.

Romans 6v23
For the wages of sin is death; but the gift of God is

eternal life through Jesus Christ our Lord.

Colossians 1v14
In whom we have redemption through his blood, even the forgiveness of sins.
Ephesians 2v13
But now in Christ Jesus ye who sometimes were far off are made nigh by the blood of Christ.

1 Peter 1v18+19

Forasmuch as ye know that ye were not redeemed with corruptible things, as silver and gold, from your vain conversation received by tradition from your fathers; But with the precious blood of Christ, as of a lamb without blemish and without spot.

Ephesians 2:8-9

For by grace are ye saved through faith; and that not of yourselves: it is the gift of God: Not of works, lest any man should boast.

Romans 10v9

That if thou shalt confess with thy mouth the Lord Jesus, and shalt believe in thine heart that God hath raised him from the dead, thou shalt be saved.

Romans 10v10

For with the heart man believeth unto right-eousness; and with the mouth confession is made unto salvation.

Romans 10v13

For whosoever shall call upon the name of the Lord shall be saved.

1 Timothy 2v5

For there is one God, and one mediator between God and men, the man Christ Jesus.

John 3v18

He that believeth on him is not condemned: but he that believeth not is condemned already, because he hath not believed in the name of the only begotten Son of God.

John 3v36

He that believeth on the Son hath everlasting life: and he that believeth not the Son shall not see life; but the wrath of God abideth on him.

Revelation 20v15

And whosoever was not found written in the book of life was cast into the lake of fire.

For God so loved the world, that he gave his only begotten Son, that whosoever believeth in him should not perish, but have everlasting life. John 3:16

www.ingramcontent.com/pod-product-compliance
Lightning Source LLC
Chambersburg PA
CBHW051051030426
42339CB00006B/304

* 9 7 8 1 7 3 7 1 0 0 5 1 5 *